I want to know all about puppies so I can help to look after our pet.

Here's what I have found out.

Dogs are **friendly** and **loving** and make great pets. A dog becomes part of the family and loves to go out with you. You must **train** it to behave well.

Dogs need lots of looking after and should not be left alone all day.

Dogs can live for about 13 or 14 years so we will have our pet for a long time.

There are more than 400
of dog, ranging
from little dogs, such as
terriers, to very large dogs,
such as Great Danes.

There are also lots of
mixed-breed or **mongrel**
dogs and they make
great pets too.

*Dogs have a much better sense of **smell** than we do and it is very important to them. Dogs can hear better than us, too.*

We have thought about what sort of dog we'd like. All puppies are **tiny** and cute, but we need to think about how big our dog will be when it grows up.

We will look for a puppy with clean bright eyes, clean ears and shiny fur.

We will ask to see the puppy's mum so we can make sure she is healthy.

Before we bring our puppy home we will buy some **food** and **water bowls** as well as a **collar** and **lead**. Our puppy will need a comfy **bed** to sleep in.

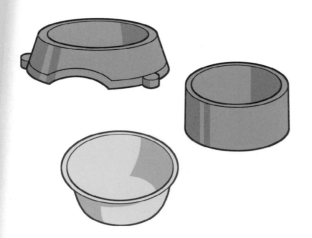

I'd like to get some **toys** too, and a brush and comb for grooming.

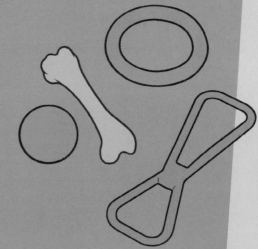

*Very important – we need a **poop scoop** for cleaning up the puppy's poo when we go out.*

A puppy is ready to leave its mum when it is about **eight weeks** old.

I will be so excited to bring our puppy home. It might be **nervous** when it first leaves its mum and brothers and sisters, so I'll be very gentle.

We will need to keep our puppy **indoors** until it has grown used to its new home.

We'll find out what our puppy likes to **eat**. Good-quality and **dog biscuits** are fine for most dogs.

I will make sure our puppy always has a bowl of fresh too.

An eight-week-old pup needs **four** meals a day. At 12 weeks, **three** meals should be enough. When our puppy is six months old, we can feed it **twice** a day.

I can give my puppy a but not too often. I know if I give my puppy too many extras it will get fat.

We will have to start **training** our new pup right away.

It won't be able to go outside until it has had its **vaccinations**. We will show the puppy where to do a wee on newspaper.

We will train our pup how to **walk** by my side and to **sit** when told to.

When I'm training my puppy I will give it lots of and never shout.

Dogs love to play and they need exercise every day.

Games such as **catch** are a great way for a dog to exercise.

But I will remember that my puppy will tire easily and must have plenty of **sleep**. I won't disturb it when it is sleeping.

I will help my puppy get used to wearing a **collar** and **lead** as soon as possible.

We have our new puppy and I love her **very** much. She is a girl and she is eight weeks old.

I will be **gentle** with our new puppy and pick her up carefully. I can put one hand under her **chest** and the other under the back of her body.

My puppy is going
to be very happy
and so am I!

Notes for parents

Care
Caring for a dog is a big responsibility. Show your child how to behave around dogs and make sure your pet has everything it needs. Your dog must have the right vaccinations and you should take it the vet if it becomes ill. You will need to find someone to look after the dog if you go on holiday without it.

Training
A dog goes out with the family and mixes with other people and animals. It is important to make sure your dog is trained and obedient. You are responsible for any mess your dog makes. Always carry a poop scoop and plastic bags when you go out with your dog.

Name tag
Make sure your dog has a tag on its collar with your contact details. Many owners also have their pet microchipped. The chip, with a special number, is injected into the skin at the back of the dog's neck. It doesn't hurt. The number can be read by a scanner if necessary.

Words to remember

breed
A type of dog, such as a German shepherd or spaniel.

mongrel
A dog that is a mix of two or more breeds.

grooming
Caring for and cleaning your dog's coat. Groom your dog by brushing and combing its coat.

vaccination
An injection given to your dog or puppy by the vet to prevent it catching certain serious illnesses.

Index